TRIPLE H

BY MATT SCHEFF

PRO WRESTLING
SUPERSTARS

Printed in the United States of America,
North Mankato, Minnesota
082013
012014

♻ THIS BOOK CONTAINS AT LEAST 10% RECYCLED MATERIALS.

Editor: Chrös McDougall
Series Designer: Jake Nordby

Photo Credits: Mel Evans/AP Images, cover, 1; Rick Scuteri/AP Images, cover (background), 1 (background), 12 (inset), 24-25, 30 (middle); Matt Roberts/Zuma Press/Icon SMI, 4-5, 10-11, 14, 31; Seth Poppel/Yearbook Library, 6; Alexandre Pona/CITYFILES/Icon SMI, 7; Daniel Kramer/ABACAUSA.COM/Newscom, 8-9; Mike Lano Photojournalism, 12-13, 17 (inset), 30 (top); Jessica Hill/AP Images, 15; Carrie Devorah/WENN/Newscom, 16-17, 28-29; Zuma Press/Icon SMI, 18-19; Chris Carlson/AP Images, 20-21; Paul Abell/AP Images for WWE, 22-23, 30 (bottom); Matt Roberts/Zuma Press/Icon SMI, 26 (inset); Alexandre Pona/CITYFILES/Icon SMI, 26-27

Library of Congress Control Number: 2013945682

Cataloging-in-Publication Data

Scheff, Matt.
  Triple H / Matt Scheff.
    p. cm. -- (Pro wrestling superstars)
  Includes index.
  ISBN 978-1-62403-140-3
  1. Triple H., 1969- --Juvenile literature. 2. Wrestlers--United States--Biography--Juvenile literature. 1. Title.
  796.812092--dc23
  [B]

                                          2013945682

CONTENTS

No Way Out **5**

Before Triple H **7**

WWE Star **12**

The Game **16**

The COO **24**

Timeline 30
Glossary 31
Index 32

Triple H is an intense competitor.

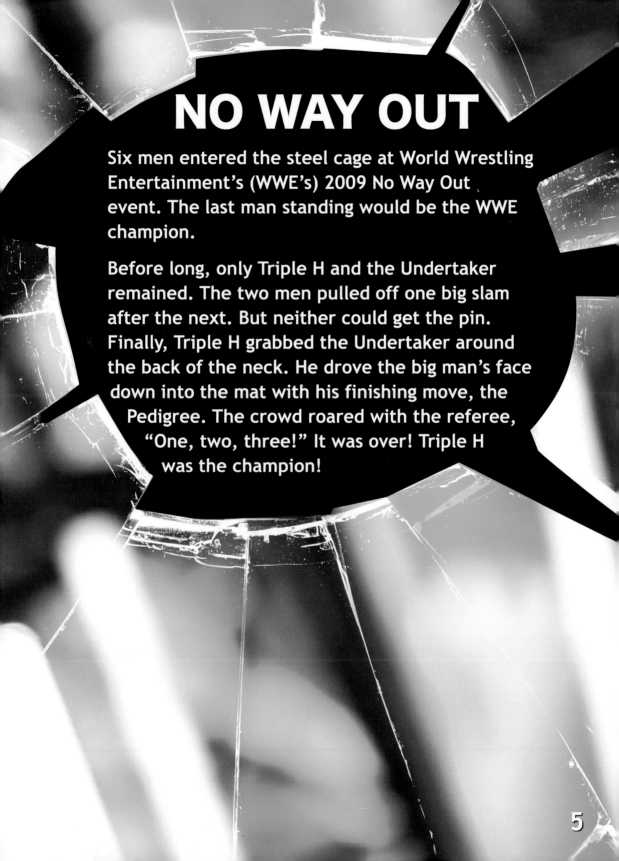

NO WAY OUT

Six men entered the steel cage at World Wrestling Entertainment's (WWE's) 2009 No Way Out event. The last man standing would be the WWE champion.

Before long, only Triple H and the Undertaker remained. The two men pulled off one big slam after the next. But neither could get the pin. Finally, Triple H grabbed the Undertaker around the back of the neck. He drove the big man's face down into the mat with his finishing move, the Pedigree. The crowd roared with the referee, "One, two, three!" It was over! Triple H was the champion!

Levesque worked hard to get his big muscles.

FAST FACT

As a kid, Levesque's favorite wrestler was Ric Flair.

BEFORE TRIPLE H

Triple H's real name is Paul Michael Levesque. He was born on July 27, 1969, in Nashua, New Hampshire. Levesque loved wrestling as a child. But he was skinny. He wanted to get stronger. So at age 14, he joined a gym. He spent his free time lifting weights.

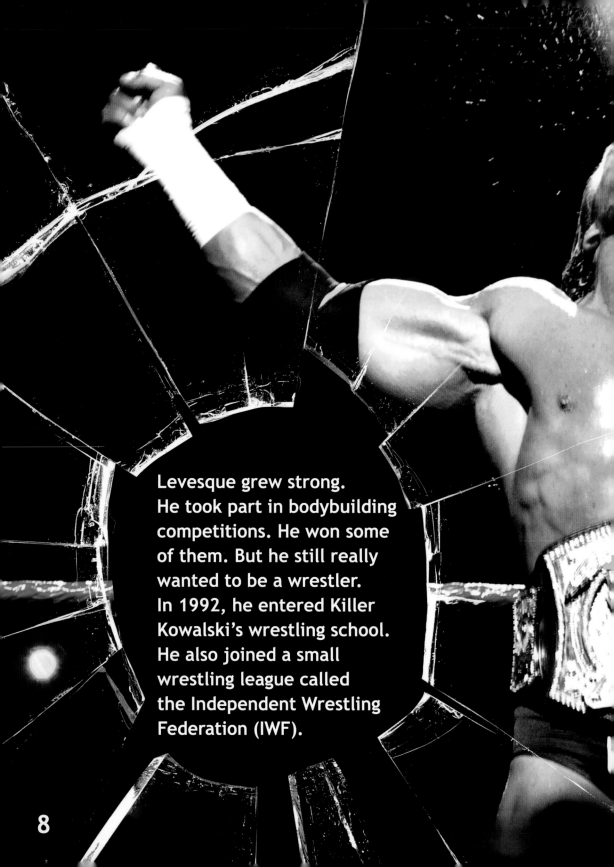

Levesque grew strong.
He took part in bodybuilding
competitions. He won some
of them. But he still really
wanted to be a wrestler.
In 1992, he entered Killer
Kowalski's wrestling school.
He also joined a small
wrestling league called
the Independent Wrestling
Federation (IWF).

Levesque was a bodybuilder before he started wrestling.

FAST FACT

Levesque's wrestling teacher, Killer Kowalski, was one of wrestling's biggest stars in the 1950s and 1960s.

In 1994, Levesque signed with World Championship Wrestling (WCW). His wrestling name was Terra Ryzing. Later he wrestled as Jean-Paul Lévesque. He pretended to be French.

WCW wanted Levesque to be a tag-team wrestler. But he wanted to wrestle singles matches. So in 1995, he left for the WWE.

Triple H stares down Randy Orton at WrestleMania 25.

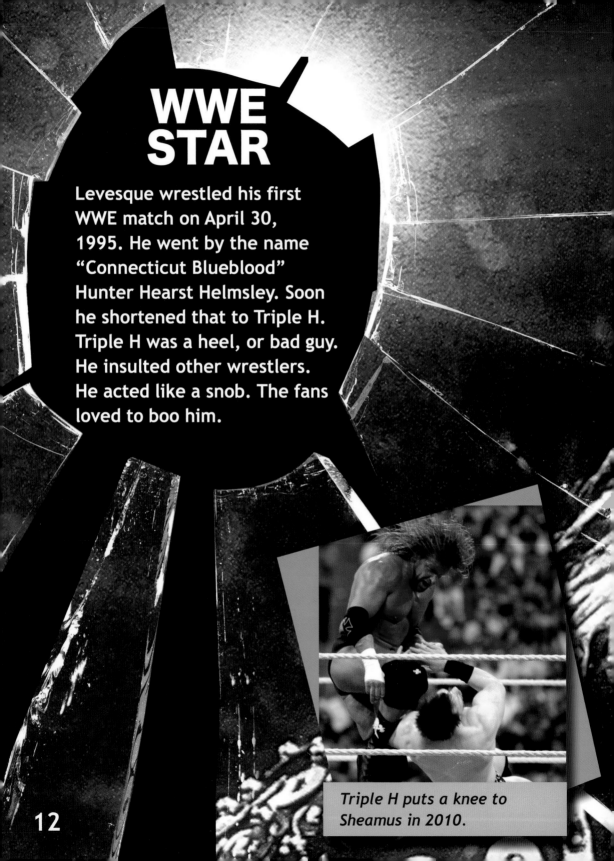

WWE STAR

Levesque wrestled his first WWE match on April 30, 1995. He went by the name "Connecticut Blueblood" Hunter Hearst Helmsley. Soon he shortened that to Triple H. Triple H was a heel, or bad guy. He insulted other wrestlers. He acted like a snob. The fans loved to boo him.

Triple H puts a knee to Sheamus in 2010.

Levesque played a rich snob early in his WWE career.

Triple H prepares to do the Pedigree on the Undertaker.

move. In 1995, Triple H developed the Pedigree. Triple H starts the Pedigree by putting his opponent's head between his knees. Then he jumps and bends his knees. The opponent's head smashes into the mat and Triple H lands on top of it. The Pedigree is a powerful move, and it helped launch Triple H to stardom.

Triple H wrestles Alberto Del Rio in 2010.

THE GAME

Triple H and Shawn Michaels led a wild group of wrestlers called D-Generation X. They dominated WWE during the late 1990s and early 2000s. Triple H won his first WWE championship in 1999. His friends Shane McMahon and the Rock helped him defeat Mankind to claim the belt. It was the first of many titles in Triple H's career.

Triple H battles Umaga.

Triple H and Shawn Michaels were part of D-Generation X.

17

Triple H gave himself the nickname "The Game." It was meant to tell the world that he was on top of the game of wrestling. He spent some time as a baby face, or good guy. But fans liked him best as a heel. He even married Stephanie McMahon, sister of Shane McMahon and daughter of hated WWE boss Vince McMahon. That made fans hate him even more!

Triple H takes on the Undertaker in 2001.

FAST FACT

Triple H was voted *Pro Wrestling Illustrated's* Most Hated Wrestler every year from 2003 to 2005.

Triple H battles Batista in 2005

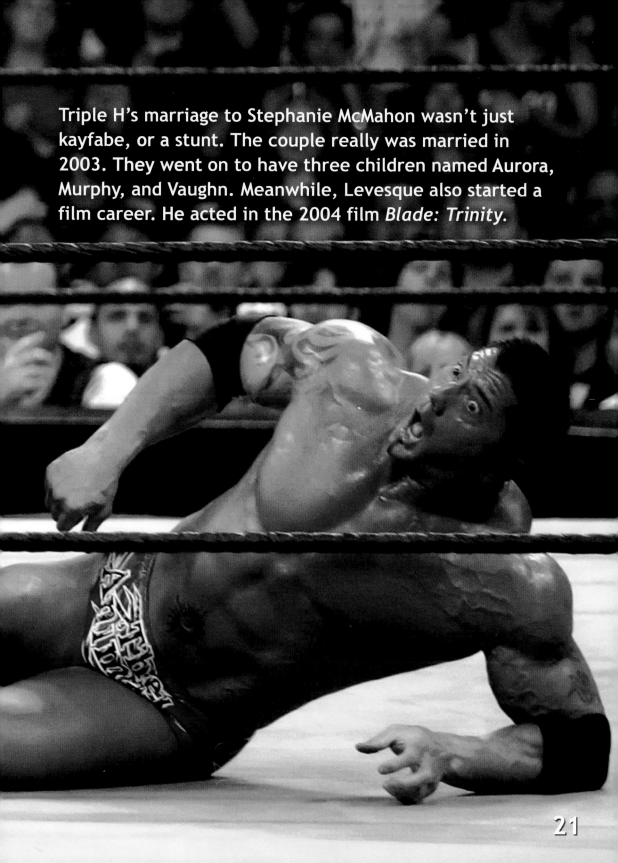

Triple H's marriage to Stephanie McMahon wasn't just kayfabe, or a stunt. The couple really was married in 2003. They went on to have three children named Aurora, Murphy, and Vaughn. Meanwhile, Levesque also started a film career. He acted in the 2004 film *Blade: Trinity*.

Triple H stares down the Undertaker.

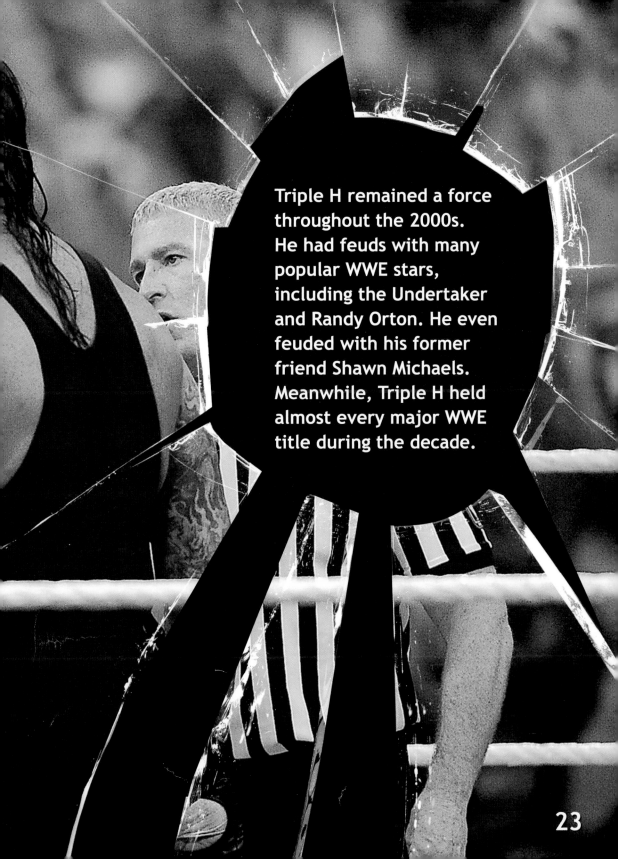

Triple H remained a force throughout the 2000s. He had feuds with many popular WWE stars, including the Undertaker and Randy Orton. He even feuded with his former friend Shawn Michaels. Meanwhile, Triple H held almost every major WWE title during the decade.

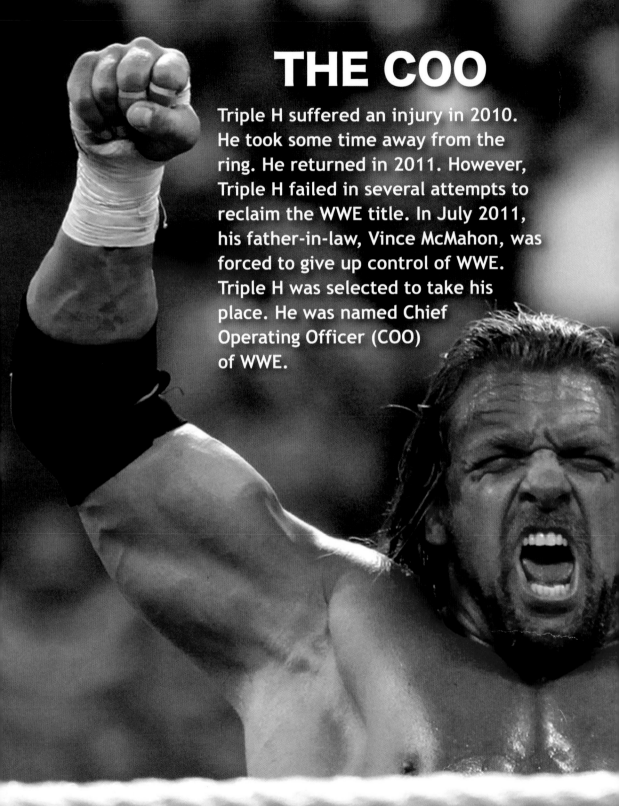

THE COO

Triple H suffered an injury in 2010. He took some time away from the ring. He returned in 2011. However, Triple H failed in several attempts to reclaim the WWE title. In July 2011, his father-in-law, Vince McMahon, was forced to give up control of WWE. Triple H was selected to take his place. He was named Chief Operating Officer (COO) of WWE.

Triple H gets pumped up before a match.

Triple H punches away at the Undertaker at WrestleMania in 2011.

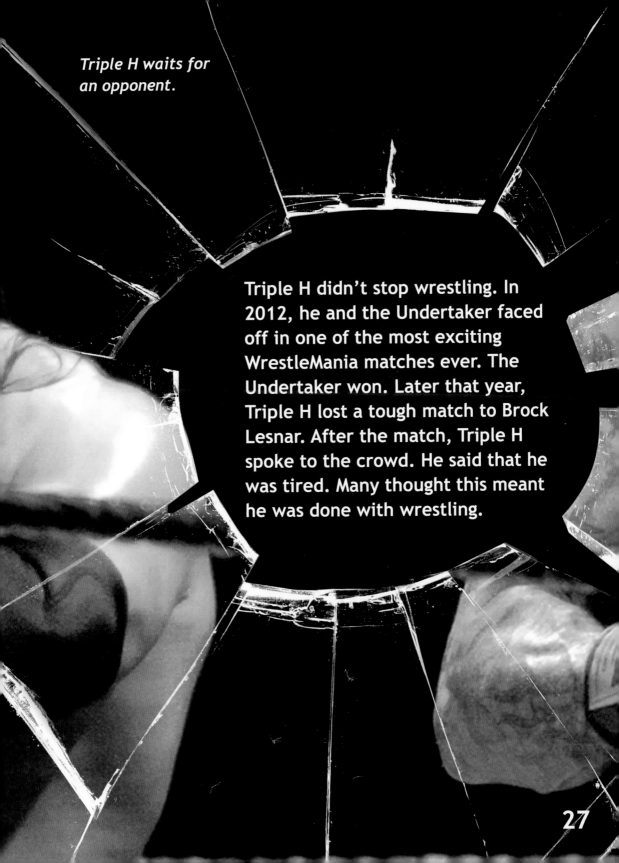

Triple H waits for an opponent.

Triple H didn't stop wrestling. In 2012, he and the Undertaker faced off in one of the most exciting WrestleMania matches ever. The Undertaker won. Later that year, Triple H lost a tough match to Brock Lesnar. After the match, Triple H spoke to the crowd. He said that he was tired. Many thought this meant he was done with wrestling.

Triple H will always be The Game.

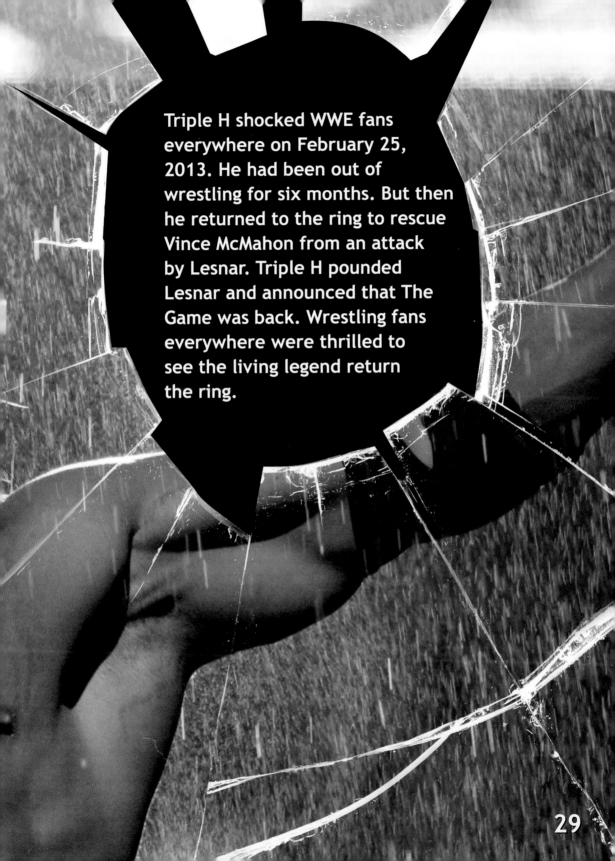

Triple H shocked WWE fans everywhere on February 25, 2013. He had been out of wrestling for six months. But then he returned to the ring to rescue Vince McMahon from an attack by Lesnar. Triple H pounded Lesnar and announced that The Game was back. Wrestling fans everywhere were thrilled to see the living legend return the ring.

1969

Paul Michael Levesque is born on July 27, 1969, in Nashua, New Hampshire.

1992

Levesque enters Killer Kowalski's wrestling school.

1994

Levesque joins WCW under the name Terra Ryzing.

1995

Levesque switches to WWE and becomes Triple H.

2003

Levesque marries Stephanie McMahon.

2004

Levesque acts in the film *Blade: Trinity*.

2011

Levesque is named COO of WWE.

2013

After being out of wrestling for six months, Triple H returns to the ring.

GLOSSARY

baby face
A wrestler whom fans view as a good guy.

bodybuilding
The act of building muscles through exercise, especially weightlifting.

chief operating officer
The person in charge of running the day-to-day operations of a business.

feud
An intense, long-lasting conflict between two wrestlers.

finishing move
A powerful move that a wrestler uses to finish off an opponent.

heel
A wrestler whom fans view as a villain.

kayfabe
In pro wrestling, the portrayal of staged situations as real.

Pedigree
Triple H's finishing move. Triple H puts an opponent's head between Triple H's knees and slams the opponent's face into the mat.

INDEX

Batista, 20
Blade: Trinity, 21
bodybuilding, 8, 9

Championships, 4, 5, 16, 23
chief operating officer (COO), 24
children, 21

D-Generation X, 16, 17
Del Rio, Alberto, 15

Early career, 8–10
early life, 6-8

Flair, Ric, 6

Independent Wrestling Federation (IWF), 8

Kowalski, Killer, 8, 9

Lesnar, Brock, 27, 29

Mankind, 16
McMahon, Shane, 16, 21
McMahon, Stephanie, 18, 21
McMahon, Vince, 18, 24, 25, 29
Michaels, Shawn, 16, 17, 23

Nashua, New Hampshire, 7
No Way Out, 5

Orton, Randy, 11, 23

Pro Wrestling Illustrated, 19

Sheamus, 12

The Pedigree, 5, 14, 15
The Rock, 16
The Undertaker, 5, 14, 19, 22, 23, 26, 27

Umaga, 17

World Championship Wrestling (WCW), 10
World Wrestling Entertainment (WWE), 4, 5, 10, 12, 13, 15, 16, 18, 23, 24, 25, 29
WrestleMania, 11, 26, 27